Lionel Kubwimana

© 2023 Ndakunda Ikirundi
Dépôt légal : Août 2021
ISBN 978-2-492960-07-9
Imprimé à la demande par Amazon
Loi n° 49-956 du 16 juillet 1949 sur les publications destinées à la jeunesse

gusinzira

to sleep – dormir

kwoga

to take a bath - prendre un bain

kwavura

to crawl - ramper

gukina

to play – jouer

kwicara

to sit – s'asseoir

kurira

to cry – pleurer

guhaguruka

to stand – se mettre debout

gukoma amashi

to clap - applaudir

gusoma

to read - lire

gufungura

to eat – manger

kunywa

to drink - boire

gutwenga

to laugh - rire

guhobera

to hug – câliner

gutambuka

to walk - marcher

kwiruka

to run – courir

gusoma

to kiss – embrasser

gusimba

to jump - sauter

kudigadiga

to tickle - chatouiller

gutamba

to dance – danser

guteka

to cook – cuisiner

gupfukama

to kneel - s'agenouiller

gusunika

to push - pousser

gukwega

to pull - tirer

kwandika
to write – écrire

kururimba

to sing - chanter

Thank you

I just wanted to thank you for purchasing this book. You are assisting my work, for which I am extremely grateful.

The best way to support me is through a review on Amazon. Your feedback assists me in better understanding your needs.
It also helps me to create and publish more books that will support the learning of Kirundi for bilingual children of all ages.

Thank you in advance for your help.

You can scan the following QR code or go to the link below to access the reviews on Amazon.

https://www.amazon.com/review/create-review?&asin=2492960072

In the same collection
Dans la même collection

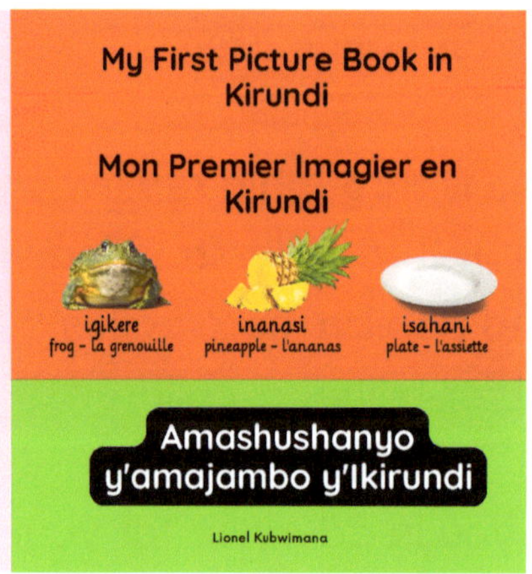

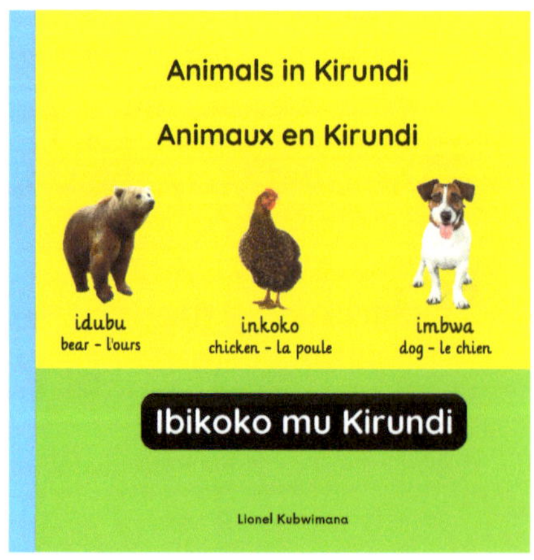

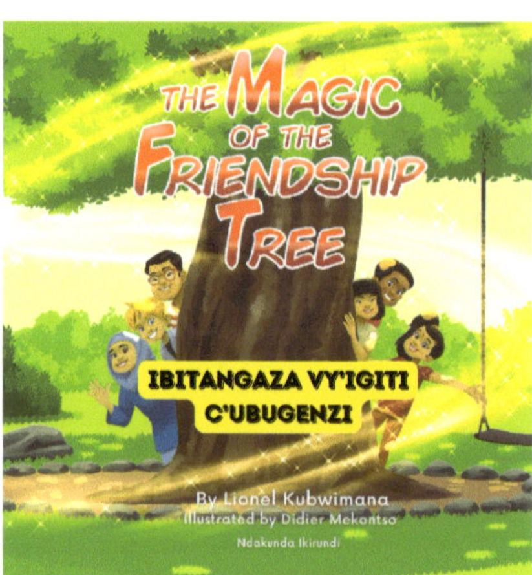

Accédez aux enregistrements audios des mots en scannant ce QR code.

Access the audio recordings of the words by scanning this QR code.